DO IT YOURSELF CREDIT REPAIR WORKBOOK

HOW TO REPAIR YOUR CREDIT IN 7 EASY STEPS

Barbara Garrett

Raleigh, NC

Published by:

GOLD BAG COMMUNICATIONS, LLC

ISBN: **978-0991382507**

ISBN-10: 0991382501

Library of Congress Cataloging in Publication Data
Washington, DC 20559

US Copyright Office   FORM TX: TXu-1-284-520
Washington, DC 20559

Garrett, Barbara A.   Date: 2009

Do It yourself Credit Repair Workbook / Barbara A. Garrett
     How to Repair your Credit in 7 easy steps

Printed in the United States

ACKNOWLEDGEMENT

I thank God for inspiring me to write this book. I thank God for allowing me to experience all the good in life and to over come all the challenges I have faced. God's love is sustaining me, and his grace is empowering me.

I also thank all my friends and family for their support

To my daughters Natalia & Alicia who are my cheerleaders
To David: My father for being a strong and loving leader in our family. He took care of all of us, including our extended family.
To Donna Richardson a tried and true friend
To my friends Diana and Julio Hasbun who are very loving and supportive.

.

I thank you all for your help.

PREFACE

This book is intended to help you repair your credit. I would like to help you repair your credit inexpensively by showing you how to do it yourself. Why pay someone to do this for you? If you have access to a computer you can reproduce the sample letters herein for your personal use or use the fill in the blank letters and mail to the appropriate credit bureau(s), creditor(s), or FTC office.

It is very difficult to live in this society with bad credit.
   Bad credit can cause you to:
   - miss out on a great career or job
   - miss your promotion at work
   - lose your job
   - miss your dream home
   - miss the car you always wanted
   - pay higher insurance rates
     o on your car, home-owners, and property insurance
   - pay hundreds of thousands of dollars in high interest rates
   - and much more

Employers pull a credit report and a criminal background record when investigating applicants for a job. The applicant may not have any criminal charges, but a bad credit rating is just as bad as being a convicted criminal. A person with bad credit is viewed as dishonest. When someone borrows money, and do not pay it back. It is stealing. These applicants with bad credit are viewed by the employer as a risk. Employers are looking for ways to cut their risk; an employee with bad credit is considered high risk. High risk employees are likely to cause an employer money. Employees with a bad credit history can cause employers money in many ways; such as, un-necessary lost time from work, employee theft, dishonesty in business handling of customers, and fraudulent claims on workers compensation or disability. The list goes on and on. You may say to yourself, "I do not handle cash money or financial information on my job". It does not matter if your job does not require you to handle money or finances, a credit report will be apart of the background investigation.

This book can be the beginning of a new life of success for you and your family. A great and successful life of prosperity awaits you because of your good credit.

Act now, the choice is yours.

THIS BOOK...

This Book is not intended to be your legal counsel. If you are being sued you need to get legal help from a professional.

The author and the publisher shall be held harmless from any failed attempts of repairing ones credit while using this workbook.

The author and the publisher make no guarantees regarding this book.

The author has used these steps to improve her own credit to a satisfactory score.

The purpose of this book is to be used as a guide; and to offer resources and references to help anyone repairing their own credit.

This book is not the final word in the credit repair business. By no means is this workbook, "the BE all and KNOW all of the credit repair industry".

The material in this book is only as current as the last copy right date

If you find the above statements unsatisfactory, and do not wish to be bound by these statements please return the book to the publisher for a full refund.

I trust you will find this book educational, helpful, and entertaining.

GOOD LUCK

TABLE OF CONTENTS

IMPORTANT ADDRESSES

CREDIT BUREAU ADDRESSES

EXPERIAN:
888-322-5583 SCORE INFORMATION—OR—800-583-4080

Inquiry Address
Experian Credit Agency
National Consumer Assist Ctr
PO Box 2002
Allen, TX 75013

Dispute Address:
Experian Credit Agency
National Consumer Asst Ctr
PO Box 9595
Allen, TX 75013

Experian Website:
www.experian.com

TRANSUNION:
800-916-8800—OR—800-888-4213

Inquiry Address
TransUnion LLC
Consumer Disclosure Ctr
P.O. Box 1000
Chester, PA 19022

Dispute Address
TransUnion, LLC
Consumer Ctr Disputes
PO Box 2000
Chester, PA 19022

TransUnion Website:
www.transunion.com

EQUIFAX:
800-797-7005

Inquiry Address
Equifax Credit Svcs, Inc.
Disclosure Department
P.O. Box 740241
Atlanta, GA 30374

Dispute Address
Equifax Information Svcs, LLC.
Disputes
PO Box 740256
Atlanta, GA 30374

Equifax Website:
www.equifax.com

ANNUAL CREDIT REPORT REQUEST SERVICE

877-FACT-ACT
Annual Credit Report
P. O. BOX 105281
ATLANTA, GA 30348
Annual Credit Report Request Service Website:
www.annualcreditreport.com

FTC ADDRESS:
FEDERAL TRADE COMMISSION

Southeast Region
Federal Trade Commission
Suite 1500
225 Peachtree Street., NE
Atlanta, GA 30303.

For Consumer Complaints contact the Consumer Response Center:

By phone: toll free 877-FTC-HELP (382-4357); 9:00 am to 5:00 pm Eastern Standard Time, Monday through Friday;

By mail:
Consumer Response Center
Federal Trade Commission
600 Pennsylvania Ave, NW,
Washington, DC 20580;

or
The Internet, using the online complaint form.

Resources:
www.ftc.gov
www.experian.com
www.equifax.com
www.transunion.com

The last few pages of this booklet contain some of the rules governing the credit bureaus. For more information on FTC rules and regulations go to www.ftc.gov

THE STEPS

HOW TO REPAIR YOUR CREDIT IN 7 EASY STEPS

1 st

STEP

The Schedule

Below is a sample schedule. It is designed to help you get organized while cleaning up your credit. This is a good way of keeping track of letters (correspondence) you have sent out to creditors and the credit bureaus; and the responses you receive back from them. Place the schedule on your refrigerator or your cork board, and update it each time you send out a letter and each time you receive a response from your letter.

- Use the sample schedule below as a guide on how to use this form:

- Use the schedule form on the following page to keep a record of all letters you sent out, and to whom you sent them.

- Review and update your schedule regularly to stay on track.
  - Do not be alarmed if you are late responding to a letter. The important thing to remember is respond regardless of how late you are.

Sample, schedule (see below)

Date sent/mailed	Addressed To:	Letter Type	Response Received	Comments/Notes
12/1/08	Equifax	Request	Yes	Received credit report 12/15/08
12/1/08	TransUnion	Dispute	Yes	Received response 12/9/08
1/10/09	Dr. Milo Kilo	Paid-off	No, receipt received	Use check#401 copy as proof paid 1/18/09
1/19/09	Experian	Paid-off	No	Did not receive updated credit file
2/22/09	FTC	Telling/ Advising	Not necessary	Reported Experian and Dr Kilo to FTC
2/26/09	No letter sent out	New credit file rec	Yes	Finally credit report is correct

Your Schedule

Date sent/mailed	Addressed To:	Letter Type	Response Received	Comments/Notes

ORDER A COPY OF YOUR CREDIT REPORT AND FICO SCORE from all three credit bureaus (Equifax, TransUnion, and Experian). You are eligible to receive a free credit report yearly from each credit bureau. You can order all three credit reports for **free** online at **www.annualcreditreport.com**, or write to the Annual Credit Report address on page 14 (if you write for a free credit report—use the request form on the following page), or call 877-FACT-ACT. The **FACT-Act** is the Fair and Accurate Credit Transactions Act; it was signed into law December 2003. The FACT Act is an amendment of the Fair Credit Reporting Act also known as the FCRA. The **FCRA** are the laws set forth by the United States government regulated by the FTC to make sure that the credit bureaus and the creditors report correct and accurate information regarding your credit worthiness. The **FTC** is the Federal Trade Commission they are the enforcers of the FCRA. If you have already requested a free credit report for the year, and it is 91 days old or older you will need to order a new credit report before beginning this process. Use the template letter named, "**Request**" on the following page to request another credit report from each credit bureau or you can buy a 3 in 1 credit report online from any of the three credit bureaus website. See page 10 for the credit bureaus web addresses.

A **FICO** score is a rating of your credit worthiness. The FICO score can range from 300 to 900. The higher your FICO score the better. The credit bureaus use the credit information they get from creditors, to grade you based on your payment history. **Creditors** are companies that lend you money or give you merchandise on credit. For example, you get the money or the merchandise now and pay later. If your grade or FICO score is 540 you are a risk; you will end up with a high interest rate. If your score is 786 you are considered good, and will have a lower interest rate. Below is an illustration of how interest rates work:

Illustration 1.1

It cost $17,000.00 to by a 2009 Honda Civic financed for 60 months with zero down payment. See how your credit score affects your monthly payments.

www.myfico.org

Credit Score	Interest Rate	Monthly Payment
412	No car	Do not qualify
548	17.514%	$898
786	6.575%	$767

Please note in the illustration above that the lower your FICO score the higher your monthly payments. The person with the low FICO score ends up paying an extra $131.00 per month which adds up to be $1,572.00 a year; and over a 5 (five) year period it is $7,860.00. This means you pay a lot more for your car compared to someone with good credit.

Below is an illustration of the FICO score range.

Illustration 1.2

CREDIT FICO SCORE RANGE AND GRADE

Grade	FICO Score
Excellent—A	750 & above
Good—B	660-749
Fair—C	620-659
Poor—D	& below-619

www.myfico.org

Remember to use a copy the fill in the blank forms on the next few pages, and put your information in the blanks to send directly to the credit bureau to request your credit report. Add a notation to your schedule on the refrigerator that you are requesting your credit report.

EQUIFAX   experian   ⫶TransUnion

Annual Credit Report Request Form

You have the right to get a free copy of your credit file disclosure, commonly called a credit report, once every 12 months, from each of the nationwide consumer credit reporting companies - Equifax, Experian and TransUnion.

For instant access to your free credit report, visit www.annualcreditreport.com.

For more information on obtaining your free credit report, visit www.annualcreditreport.com or call 877-322-8228.

Use this form if you prefer to write to request your credit report from any, or all, of the nationwide consumer credit reporting companies. The following information is required to process your request. Omission of any information may delay your request.

Once complete, fold (do not staple or tape), place into a #10 envelope, affix required postage and mail to:

Annual Credit Report Request Service P.O. Box 105281 Atlanta, GA 30348-5281.

Please use a Black or Blue Pen and write your responses in PRINTED CAPITAL LETTERS without touching the sides of the boxes like the examples listed below:

A B C D E F G H I J K L M N O P Q R S T U V W X Y Z   0 1 2 3 4 5 6 7 8 9

Social Security Number:

Date of Birth:

Month   Day   Year

- - - - - Fold Here - Fold Here - - - - -

First Name   M.I.

Last Name   JR, SR, III, etc.

Current Mailing Address:

House Number   Street Name

Apartment Number / Private Mailbox   For Puerto Rico Only: Print Urbanization Name

City   State   ZipCode

Previous Mailing Address (complete only if at current mailing address for less than two years):

House Number   Street Name

- - - - - - - - - - - - - - - Fold Here - Fold Here - - - - - - - -

Apartment Number / Private Mailbox   For Puerto Rico Only: Print Urbanization Name

City   State   ZipCode

Shade Circle Like This → ● Not Like This → ⊗ ⊘	I want a credit report from (shade each that you would like to receive): ○ Equifax ○ Experian ○ TransUnion

○ Shade here if, for security reasons, you want your credit report to include no more than the last four digits of your Social Security Number.

31238

If additional information is needed to process your request, the consumer credit reporting company will contact you by mail.

Your request will be processed within 15 days of receipt and then mailed to you.

Copyright 2004, Central Source LLC

23

THE REQUEST LETTER

1308 Sweet Pea Road
Raleigh, NC 27610
March 1, 2009

Equifax Credit Information Services, Inc.
Disclosure Department
P.O. Box 740241
Atlanta, GA 30374

To Whom It May Concern:

Please mail me a copy of my credit report. I have applied for Credit with several Financial Companies in my area, and was denied credit. I have attached a copy of my North Carolina Drivers License and my Social Security card. Please note my information below to ensure that I receive the correct credit report:

Name:	Barbara Garrett
Address:	1308 Sweet Pea Road, Raleigh, NC 27610
Telephone #:	919-555-1212
Social Security #:	123-45-6789
Date of Birth:	June 2, 1969

If any further information is needed please feel free to call me at home most days before 12 noon.

Sincerely,

Barbara Garrett
Consumer

THE REQUEST LETTER
Fill in the Blanks Request

_____
Address

_____
City, ST Zipcode

_____
Date

_____
Name Credit Bureau

Disclosure Department

_____
Address

_____
City, ST Zipcode

To Whom It May Concern:

Please mail me a copy of my credit report. I have applied for Credit with several Financial Companies in my area, and was denied credit. I have attached a copy of my North Carolina Drivers License and my Social Security card. Please note my information below to ensure that I receive the correct credit report:

Name:	_____
Address:	_____
Telephone #:	_____
Social Security #:	_____
Date of Birth:	_____

If any further information is needed please feel free to call me at home most days around _____.

Sincerely,

_____   _____
Sign   Print Name
Consumer

2nd

STEP

REVIEW YOUR CREDIT REPORT. **Next prepare a letter challenging and disputing all derogatory information listed on the credit report that does not belong to you.** If you find all the information is correct on the credit report ask the credit bureau to verify all accounts for accuracy. **BE SURE** to include your credit report number in the letter. Use the letter template named, "**Dispute**" on the following page as an example.

You have a choice when disputing derogatory information:

- You can file a dispute online with the credit bureaus on their websites or

- Write a letter by typing the letter or use the fill in the blank form letter on the next few pages to dispute the derogatory information on your credit report.

It is best to write a letter because you may need to report the credit bureau(s) to the overseer (the FTC) for not following the law and rules. Writing a letter is your proof you submitted a dispute to the credit bureau. This process is known as creating a paper trail in business. Take a moment when visiting the credit bureaus websites and try to find an address to submit your dispute in writing. It is next to impossible to find a consumer service center dispute address. There is a reason for this. The credit bureaus do not want you to write them. They discourage you from writing letters. Letters leave a paper trail which results in them being accountable. Your letter is your proof you have submitted a dispute. It is like a receipt. Imagine submitting a dispute online, and it gets lost in cyber-space never to been seen again. If you are trying to buy a house or make a large purchase time is critical.

*Here is a **reminder:** Copy and use (over and over again) the fill in the blank letters on the next few pages to put your information, and mail the fill in the blank letter directly to the credit bureaus. Review your schedule, put today's date on your schedule, and note what you mailed out.*

On the next page is an example of a credit report. This example can help you understand your credit report when you get it in the mail.

CREDIT REPORT ABBREVIATIONS & MEANINGS

Loan Type Abbreviations	
MN Open/Monthly Account. An account to be paid in full after each billing.	**IN** Installment Account: An account with a fixed number of specified payments. Mortgages or car loan for example.
RV Revolving account. An account with regular monthly payments on the balance due. Such as credit cards.	**UN** Unknown account. An account with an unknown loan type.
OT Other companies account being collected. Usually indicates a collection agency.	

Payment Record Codes				
Loan Type	**MN**	**IN**	**RV**	**UN**
Too new to rate. Approved but unused	O0	I0	R0	U0
Pays (or paid) within 30 days. Pays as agreed	O1	I1	R1	U1
Pays (or paid) in more than 30 but less than 60 days	02	I2	R2	U2
Pays (or paid) in more than 60 but less than 90 days	O3	I3	R3	U3
Pays (or paid) in more than 90 but less than 120 days	O4	I4	R4	U4
Account at least 120 days overdue, yet to go to collection	O5	I5	R5	U5
Wage earner plan or similar payment agreement	O7	I7	R7	U7
Repossession	O8	I8	R8	U8
Bad debt, placed for collection, skip	O9	I9	R9	U9

Equal Credit Opportunity Act (ECOA) Codes and Definitions	
Undesignated-0 Individual's association with this account is unknown	**Individual -1** Individual has contractual responsibility for this account
Joint Account-Contractual Responsibility-2 Individual has contractual responsibility for this account. There may be others who also have contractual responsibility for this account.	**Joint Account- Authorized User-3** Individual is only authorized to use this account. Someone else has contractual responsibility.

SAMPLE CREDIT REPORT

Equifax Style

```
EQUIFAX CREDIT base

I Dayton,Dave*
2 149,,Jefferson,,Fantasy Island,IL,60750*
5 124541982,,,**
TYPTS,EU-RentScreeners Inc,ALG002

//////////////////////        CREDITbase AnyBureau Report   //////////////////////
//////////////////////        Equifax-Style Report Generated from Trans Union Data
//
// End User: RentScreeners Inc                              //
// Operator: DEF            Data Timestamp: 08/04/98 15:46 //
///////////////////////////////////////////////// Printed: 12/22/98 11:36 //

***EMPIRICA ALERT: SCORE +00668:      022/010/008/014 ***

*DAYTON,DAVE Since        FAD
 149 JEFFERSON,FANTASY ISLAND IL 60750
 SSS-124-54-1982
 01 ES-,ABC BANK
**************************************************
*INQS-Subject Shows 08 Inquiries Since 08/24/97
    MERIT SYST ZLA8256407 08/04/98    HOUSEHOLD Y111992043 02/05/98
    CBC CO MAC ZLG0076311 02/05/98    1000 OAKS ZLA0085124 01/07/98
    MERIT SYST ZLA8256407 01/05/98    CBC CO MAC ZLG0076311 01/05/98
    GMAC MORT FRD0091736 10/03/97     TMS-HIRCA QST1960042 08/24/97

C O L L E C T I O N S
  Firm/ID Code      OPND  VRFD   CLSD   $Placed Balance CS ECOA Account
Number
ABLE ASSOC 91MY001          M      $1200 $1200  O9B I 12345
  Creditor-ABC BANK, Remarks-Placed For Collection
ABLE ASSOC 91MY001          M      $1300 $1300  O9B I 123456
  Creditor-ABC BANK, Remarks-Placed For Collection
ABLE ASSOC 91MY001          M      $1400 $1400  O9B I 1234567
  Creditor-ABC BANK, Remarks-Placed For Collection

T R A D E S
*  Firm/ID Code     RPTD OPND H/C TRM  BAL P/D CS  MR ECOA Account Number
CHOICE   1679002         2414    543   R01     I 809098
  30( )60( )90+( ) Verified V
SIMMONS FN 1067003          125 P12  0     I01    I 1287009817
  30( )60( )90+( ) Verified V
BTMN'S BK  8758006          20Q 4433    I01    I 9898009876
  30( )60( )90+( ) Verified V

End Of Report -        -- Serviced By:

FANTASY ISLAND / 0605 TEST MARKET              800 888-4213
555 W. ADAMS CHICAGO, IL. 60661
```

http://www.consumerinfo.com/n/expsam.htm

REPAIR YOUR CREDIT

THE DISPUTE LETTER

Date: March 2, 2009

From: Barbara Garrett
             1308 Sweet Pea Rd
             Raleigh, NC 27610

To: Experian Credit Agency
             National Consumer Assistance Center
             PO Box 9595
             Allen, TX 75013

Subject: Credit Report # 2345678901

To Whom It May Concern,

Please verify the accounts listed below: I believe these accounts are listed on my credit report in error.

       ACME Wood Company, Reading, PA
       Dr. Kilo Milo, Washington, DC
       Regional Acceptance Corp., Chicago, IL
       First National, Inc., Raleigh, NC

Please send me an up-to-date credit report showing all accounts verified and corrected.

I can be reached at the address above or by telephone at 919-555-1212.

Sincerely,

Barbara Garrett
Consumer

THE DISPUTE LETTER
Fill in the Blanks Dispute

Date: _____

From: _____
Name

_____
Address

_____
City, ST Zipcode

To: _____
Name Credit Bureau

National Consumer Center, Dispute Dept.

_____
Address

_____
City, ST Zipcode

Subject: Credit Report # _____

To Whom It May Concern,

Please verify the accounts listed below: I believe these accounts are listed on my credit report in error.
1. _____
2. _____
3. _____
4. _____

Please send me an up-to-date credit report showing all accounts verified and corrected.

I can be reached at the address above or by telephone at 919-555-1212.

Sincerely,

_____   _____
Sign   Print Name

3rd

STEP

DID YOU RECEIVE YOUR UP-TO-DATE CREDIT REPORTS FROM THE CREDIT BUREAUS, SINCE DISPUTING AND VERIFYING ALL THE BAD STUFF???

IF YES,

Make a notation on your schedule that you received your up-to-date credit report, and go to step 4

IF NO,

proceed with the instructions below.

The creditors and credit bureaus are required by law to respond to your letter with in 30 days. If they fail to respond they are in violation of breaking the law according to the FCRA. You **must** report them to the FTC to be punished for breaking the law. Therefore, on day 32 **WRITE TWO LETTERS** (and record it on your schedule).

- Write a letter to the FTC, and
- Write a letter to each credit bureau that did not send you an updated credit report.

The FTC is the overseer or the police (5-0) over the credit bureaus and creditors. The FTC has the power to access fines and penalties against the creditors and the credit bureaus. The FTC makes sure that the credit bureaus and creditors follow the FCRA (Fair Credit Reporting Act). The FCRA is the like the Bible of what the credit bureaus and creditors can and cannot do regarding consumer credit. Tell the FTC by letter that the credit bureaus broke the law. They (the credit bureaus) are in violation of not responding to your dispute within 30 days. Use the letter template named, "**FTC—1**" on the next few pages to compose your letter. Also, write a letter to the credit bureaus informing them that you have reported them to the FTC, use the letter template named, "**Telling—1**" on the following pages.

Remember *you can copy the fill in the blank template; and write your information in the blanks, and send directly to the FTC and the credit bureau. Also, make a note and review your schedule that you mailed these letters today.*

Very Important: Send your attachments and copies of letters you sent to the credit bureau to the FTC when reporting them for failure to respond within 30 days.

REPAIR YOUR CREDIT

FTC -1 LETTER

Barbara Garrett
1308 Sweet Pea Road
Raleigh, NC 27610
March 4, 2009

Southeast Region
Federal Trade Commission
Suite 1500
225 Peachtree Street, NE
Atlanta, GA 30303.

Subject: Credit Report # 2345678901

To Whom It May Concern:

I have disputed several items on the above mentioned credit report. I have not received a response regarding the disputed information from Equifax. It has been 35 days since I have submitted my dispute. See the attached dispute letter I sent to Equifax. Please fine Equifax the maximum penalty for not responding.

Sincerely,

Barbara Garrett
Consumer

FTC –1 LETTER
Fill in the Blanks FTC—1

_____
Name
_____
Address
_____
City, ST Zipcode
_____
Date

Southeast Region
Federal Trade Commission
Suite 1500
225 Peachtree Street, NE
Atlanta, GA 30303.

Subject: _____

To Whom It May Concern:

I have disputed several items on the above mentioned credit report. I have not received a response regarding the disputed information from _____. It has been 35 plus days since I have submitted my dispute. See the attached dispute letter I sent to _____. Please fine _____ the maximum penalty for not responding.

Sincerely,

_____   _____
Sign   Print Name
Consumer

FTC—1 TELLING

Date: March 6, 2009

From:
Barbara Garrett
1308 Sweet Pea Road
Raleigh, NC 27610

To:
Equifax Credit Bureau
PO Box 740256
Atlanta, GA 30374

Subject: Credit Report # 2345678901

To Whom It May Concern:

Please be advised that I have reported you to the FTC for not responding to my dispute letter regarding my credit record. Please, see the attached letter I have sent to the FTC showing proof that you are in violation of the FCRA.

Sincerely,

Barbara Garrett
Concern Consumer

FTC −1 TELLING

Fill in the Blanks FTC—1 Telling

Date: _____

_____
From:

_____
Name

_____
Address

_____
City, ST Zipcode

To:

_____
Credit bureau or creditor

_____
Department Info

_____
Address

_____
City, ST. Zipcode

Subject: Credit Report _____

To Whom It May Concern:

Please be advised that I have reported you to the FTC for not responding to my dispute letter regarding my credit record. Please, see the attached letter I have sent to the FTC showing proof that you are in violation of the FCRA.

Sincerely,

_____   _____
Sign   Print Name
Consumer

STEP 4—Pay off all outstanding debt

4th

STEP

Pay off all outstanding debt. Use the credit report you received from the credit bureaus since submitting your dispute/verification letter to begin paying off your bad, delinquent, and outstanding debt. As you begin to pay off the bad debt—start with the smallest debt first, and then work your way up to the larger debt. Paying off the small debt begins to build better credit immediately. Contact all creditors on the credit report with derogatory information about you, and begin negotiating a pay off. A good rule of thumb to follow is start with an offer around 40% to pay-off bad debt, for example, if you owe $1,000.00 offer to pay $400.00, and keep negotiating until you are satisfied. It is a good idea to have cash ready to pay off debt; try not to do a payment plan unless absolutely necessary. Below are some ideas on getting your hands on some cash:

- Refinance your vehicle if it has value or is paid off
- Refinance your home or other valuables
- Sell items of value to a pawn shop or sell those items on e-bay for quick money
- Use your savings
- Take a loan against your savings; for instance, a loan against your 401k, or certificate of deposit, etc.

- Take out a loan if possible from friends, family, or a finance company to have cash ready to pay off bad debt.

- Get a part time job or see if you can get overtime on your current job.

Once you have paid off a debt get a receipt from the creditor. If you do not receive a receipt use the following as a replacement receipt:

- Cancelled check from your bank

- Visa/Mastercard check card confirmation number and copy of the transaction posting to your bank account

- Money order stubs as proof you paid the creditor. Buy your money orders from the USPS (US Postal Service) because the USPS is a government facility, and the government keeps great records. In the event you need to have a trace put on the money order. Convenience stores and corner stores are ok, but it could take weeks or months to get confirmation that a money order was cashed.

Next ask the creditor(s) to update your credit record to show that this debt is paid in full. Use the letter template named, "**Paid-off**" to prepare a letter to send to each credit bureau with attached copies of all receipts of paid off debt from all creditors. Ask the credit bureaus to update your credit file showing the debt as paid in full with a zero balance, and mail you an updated credit report.

If you have filed bankruptcy and it has been dismissed or discharged contact the clerk of the Bankruptcy court in your area to have the status of your bankruptcy listed/published on your credit report. In-addition, mail copies of your bankruptcy dismissal or bankruptcy discharge to each credit bureau to have your credit report updated.

If you have judgments against you, and it has been satisfied, discharged, or dismissed use the same process to get your credit report up to date. Again, contact the clerk of court where your judgment is and have the clerk up-date your credit file regarding the status of your judgment. You will need to send in copies of your court documents to the credit bureaus showing that the judgment is either dismissed, discharged, or satisfied. Writing letters are not a waste of time.

****** DO NOT FORGET TO SEND IN SUPPORTING
DOCUMENTS WITH YOUR LETTERS TO THE CREDIT
BUREAUS AND THE FTC******

*Also at your disposal on the next few pages are the fill in the
blank letters you can write your information in the blank letters;
and send in directly to the credit bureaus, creditors, and FTC.
See the letters on the following pages. It is very important to
note and review your schedule to stay on track.*

REPAIR YOUR CREDIT

PAID-OFF LETTER

Date: March 3, 2009

From:
Barbara Garrett
1308 Sweet Pea Rd
Raleigh, NC 27610

To:
TransUnion LLC
Consumer Disclosure Disputes
P.O. Box 2000
Chester, PA 19022

Subject: Credit Report # 2345678901

To Whom It May Concern,

Please be advised that the attached letters and receipts are pay-off verification for settlements on several delinquent accounts listed on my credit report. Please update my credit record with the attached information.   The following accounts have been paid in full, and settled, see below.

SETTLED/PAID OFF DELIQUENT ACCOUNTS		
Account Name	**Company Owed**	**Account number**
ACME Wood Company, Reading, PA	ACME Wood Company, Reading, PA	215-14330301
Dr. Kilo Milo, Washington, DC	The Back Specialist, Washington, DC	543881-09855
RMA – Risk Management Assoc, Lansing, MI	Regional Acceptance Corp, Co Chicago, IL	3443731 # 00021433303
Professional Recovery Consultants, Durham, NC	First National, Inc Raleigh, NC	XRN00091275370F
Capital Medical Associates Richmond, VA	Dr. D M James-Jones, MD Richmond, VA	1690346

Please feel free to contact me at the address above or call me at home on 919-555-1212.

Sincerely,

Barbara Garrett

THE PAID-OFF LETTER
Fill in the Blanks Paid-Off

Date: _____

From: _____

Name _____

Address _____

City, ST Zipcode _____

To:

_____
Name Credit Bureau

National Consumer Center, Dispute Dept.

_____
Address

_____
City, ST Zipcode

Subject: Credit Report # _____

To Whom It May Concern,

Please be advised that the attached letters and receipts are pay-off verification for settlements on several delinquent accounts listed on my credit report. Please update my credit record with the attached information. The following accounts have been paid in full, and settled, see below.

SETTLED/PAID OFF DELIQUENT ACCOUNTS		
Account Name	**Company Owed**	**Account number**

Sincerely,

_____
Sign

_____
Print Name

5th

STEP

IT IS TELLING TIME AGAIN! DID YOU RECEIVE AN UPDATED CREDIT REPORT AFTER MAILING IN COPIES OF RECEIPTS AND COPIES OF COURT DOCUMENTATION.????

IF YES,

Again make another notation on your schedule, saying you received your updated credit report, and go to step 6

IF NO,

Proceed to the instructions below:

Once again the credit bureaus and the creditors have 30 days to contact you with their findings regarding your paid off letters. If you have not received an updated credit report it is time to prepare some more letters to the FTC informing them that the credit bureaus and the creditors are in violation of not following the rules and laws outlined in the FCRA. On the following pages are examples of letters you can use to contact the FTC. Use the letter template named, "**FTC—2**". Also, write a letter to each credit bureau and each creditor in violation of not responding to the paid off letters you submitted to them. Let them know that they (the credit bureaus and the creditors) have been reported to the FTC, use the letter template named, "**Telling—2**".

**** <ins>DO NOT FORGET TO SEND COPIES OF THE PAY OFF LETTERS AND RECIEPTS TO THE FTC!!</ins> ****

The fill in the blank letters are available in this section for you to write in your own personal information, and mail the letters directly to the creditors, credit bureau, and the FTC. Please make a copy, and use them over and over again as many times as you need. Let's review your schedule to stay on track. Make a notation on your schedule today of all letters and documents mailed out.

FTC—2 LETTER

Barbara Garrett
1308 Sweet Pea Road
Raleigh, NC 27610
March 4, 2009

Southeast Region
Federal Trade Commission
225 Peachtree Street, NE, STE 1500
Atlanta, GA 30303.

Subject: Credit Report # 2345678901

To Whom It May Concern:

Equifax, First Nation, Inc., and Regional Acceptance have been paid
in full since February 2009. I have written and called them asking
them to update my credit record regarding the pay-offs of said
accounts, but to-date my credit record still shows these accounts
as bad debt not paid. My understanding of the FTC consumer laws
states that Equifax and the creditors have a responsibility to
contact me regarding the disputed information with in 30 days.
Please fine and penalize each creditor and Equifax the maximum
for not updating my credit record.

Attached is a copy of my credit report showing the creditors'
information not updated, copies of the pay-off letters, copies of
receipts from the creditors showing account is paid, and copies of
letters to Equifax requesting my credit record to be updated.

Creditors	Address	Account #	Amount due
ACME Wood Company	236 N. Town Street, Reading, PA 19601	215-14330301	$ 0.00
Regional Acceptance Corp collection agency: RMA-Risk Alternatives, Inc.	1420 E. Firetower Rd Chicago, IL 60637 1829 Reisterstown Road Baltimore, MD 21208	3443731 reference #: 0002143303	$0.00 $0.00
Equifax Credit Bureau	PO Box 740256 Atlanta, GA 30374	Credit report # 2345678901	$0.00

Sincerely,

Barbara A. Garrett
Cc: ACME Wood Company, Regional Accept, Equifax

60

FTC—2 LETTER
Fill in the Blanks FTC—2

_____
Name

_____
Address

_____
City, ST Zipcode

_____
Date

Southeast Region
Federal Trade Commission
225 Peachtree Street, NE, STE 1500
Atlanta, GA 30303.

Subject: _____

To Whom It May Concern:

My debt with the creditor(s) listed below has been paid off since
_____. I have written and called them asking them to
update my credit record regarding the pay-offs of said accounts,
but to-date my credit record still shows these accounts as bad debt
not paid. My understanding of the FTC consumer laws states that
credit bureau(s) and the creditor(s) have a responsibility to contact
me regarding the disputed information with in 30 days. Please fine
and penalize each creditor and credit bureau the maximum for not
updating my credit record.

Attached is a copy of my credit report showing the creditors'
information not updated, copies of the pay-off letters and receipts
from the creditors, and copies of letters sent to the credit
bureau(s) requesting my credit record to be updated, and a copy of
my driver's license.

Creditors	Address	Account #	Amount due

Sincerely,

_____   _____
Sign   Print Name
Cc:

FTC—2 TELLING

Date: March 6, 2009

From:
Barbara A. Garrett
1308 Sweet Pea Road
Raleigh, NC 27610

To:

Equifax Credit	Regional Acceptance	Corp First Nat'l
PO Box 740256	1420 E. Firetower Road	236 N. Town St
Atlanta, GA 30374	Chicago, IL 60637	Reading, PA 19601

To Whom It May Concern:

Please be advised that I have reported you to the FTC for not
updating my credit record in a timely manner. Please, see the
attached letter.

Thanks,

Barbara A. Garrett
Concern Consumer

FTC—2 TELLING
Fill in the Blanks FTC—2 Telling

Date: _____

           From :

         _____

            Name

         _____

           Address

         _____

        City, ST Zipcode

To:

_____
Credit bureau or creditor

_____
Department Info

_____
Address

_____
City, ST. Zipcode

To Whom It May Concern:

Please be advised that I have reported you to the FTC for not updating my credit record in a timely manner. Please, see the attached letter.

Thanks,

_____   _____
Sign   Print
Concern Consumer

6th

STEP

Negotiate your existing accounts. If you have open accounts that are severely delinquent, showing late payments or slow payments contact the creditor(s) and try to negotiate a new payment arrangement. See below:

- Ask for more time to pay-off the loan; consider this, if you have a 36 months term loan ask if it can be extended to 42 months
- Ask for a lower interest rate?
- Ask what are your options?

You can do this yourself without the help of those companies and organizations that try to put you on a special payment plan charging lots of money to do something you can do for yourself. This is extra money that can be used to pay off some of that debt. Simply explain to the creditor(s) you are having financial difficulties, below are some typical hardships:

- going through a divorce
- getting sick and being under-insured or no medical insurance
- death of a close relative (parent, sibling, spouse, child, etc)
- losing a job or job cutting back on hours

- major appliance repair or replacement, i.e., stove, refrigerator, HVAC system

- a major car repairs (replace engine/transmission, etc.)

- car accident

- becoming disabled

- a run of bad luck, etc...the list goes on and on

Remember to notate your schedule on all the progress you have made negotiating your pay-offs. I am so proud of you.

7th
STEP

Building good credit begins with **paying all open accounts on time**. If you do not have any open accounts sign up to get a pre-paid and/or secured credit card from Capital One or some other major credit card vendor. A **secured credit card** is an account which you open and deposit money into the account and the bank holds the deposit as collateral against the credit card. A secure credit card is a way to start a new positive credit history. **<u>Pay the credit card on time every month</u>**. Wait at least 6 to 12 months before applying for any new credit. Check to ensure your FICO score is climbing higher. Sign up for a credit alert from Life Lock or pull your credit report quarterly. A credit-alert notifies you if someone or a company pulls a credit report or score inquiry on you. This credit alert will help protect you from identity theft for a small monthly fee. You can subscribe to this credit alert at the website link below: www.credit-repair-diy.com

Maximum credit score growth:

- Use no more than 30% to 50% of all credit lines available to you. Let's look at the example below, if you have a credit line of $10,000.00 use only $3,000.00 of it and keep $7,000.00 available for use, but the key is do not use the $7,000.00. Using all of your available credit, and being maxed out on every line of credit hurts your credit score. You begin to become a credit risk.

- Next, do not over extend yourself by having too many lines of credit open. A good rule to follow is no more than 10-15% of your income should go to paying credit card debt every month. Several lines of credit can hurt you when you want to purchase a house. Some creditors calculate your maximum pay out every month as if you were already maxed out. Here is how you calculate the 10-15% in relation to how much credit card debt you should have. If you make $50,000.00 per year you should have a maximum of $7,500.00 in credit card debt, any more could cause your credit score to go down.

- When closing out accounts to keep from being over extended, BE CAREFUL. BE VERY CAREFUL AND CAUTIOUS!! Evaluate all accounts to see which accounts have been open the longest. You want to keep the accounts with the longest credit history even if it has some negative reporting. You do not want to be classified as a new borrower, especially if you have several new accounts open with short credit history or no accounts at all.

Final, when shopping for a loan do not go from lender to lender putting credit applications. This is bad. Too many inquiries will bring down your credit score.

CONGRADULATIONS YOU HAVE DONE IT...YOU HAVE NOW GOT YOUR CREDIT BACK ON TRACK, AND YOUR FICO SCORE IS RISING STEADILY.

CONGRADULATONS I AM SO PROUD OF YOU.

Feel free to help friends and family get their credit back on track.

I wish you the very best, and all your dreams to come true.

Do You need rescuing?

I understand if you feel that this process is too much for you to handle. Writing all of these letters require a lot of time and energy. It is not an easy task. Believe me I sympathize with you.

I have seminars that I offer on occasion to others to repair their credit using these very step. Please go to the website below to see when the next work shop will be.

www.credit-repair-diy.com

APPENDIX I

FAIR CREDIT REPORTING ACT
FCRA
UNITED STATES CODE
§ 15 USC 1681i

TITLE 15 COMMERCE AND TRADE
CHAPTER 41 CONSUMER CREDIT PROTECTION
SUBCHAPTER III CREDIT REPORTING AGENCIES
Sec. 1681i. Procedure in case of disputed accuracy

TITLE 15 > CHAPTER 41 > SUBCHAPTER III > Sec. 1681i

(a) Reinvestigations of disputed information
(1) Reinvestigation required
          (A) In general

If the completeness or accuracy of any item of information

contained in a consumer's file at a consumer reporting

agency is disputed by the consumer and the consumer

notifies the agency directly of such dispute, the agency shall

reinvestigate free of charge and record the current status of

the disputed information, or delete the item from the file in

accordance with paragraph (5), before the end of the 30-day

period beginning on the date on which the agency receives

the notice of the dispute from the consumer.

          (2) Prompt notice of dispute to furnisher of information
                    (A) In general

Before the expiration of the 5-business-day period beginning on the date on which a consumer reporting agency receives notice of a dispute from any consumer in accordance with paragraph (1), the agency shall provide notification of the dispute to any person who provided any item of information in dispute, at the address and in the manner established with the person. The notice shall include all relevant information regarding the dispute that the agency has received from the consumer.

(B) Provision of other information from consumer

The consumer reporting agency shall promptly provide to the person who provided the information in dispute all relevant information regarding the dispute that is received by the agency from the consumer after the period referred to in subparagraph (A) and before the end of the period referred to in paragraph (1)(A).

(5) Treatment of inaccurate or unverifiable information
    (A) In general

If, after any reinvestigation under paragraph (1) of any information disputed by a consumer, an item of the information is found to be inaccurate or incomplete or cannot be verified, the consumer reporting agency shall promptly

delete that item of information from the consumer's file or

modify that item of information, as appropriate, based on the

results of the reinvestigation.

(B) Requirements relating to reinsertion of
previously deleted material
(i) Certification of accuracy of information
If any information is deleted from a consumer's file pursuant
to subparagraph (A), the information may not be reinserted
in the file by the consumer reporting agency unless the
person who furnishes the information certifies that the
information is complete and accurate.

(ii) Notice to consumer
If any information that has been deleted from a consumer's
file pursuant to subparagraph (A) is reinserted in the file, the
consumer reporting agency shall notify the consumer of the
reinsertion in writing not later than 5 business days after the
reinsertion or, if authorized by the consumer for that
purpose, by any other means available to the agency.

(iii) Additional information
As part of, or in addition to, the notice under clause (ii), a
consumer reporting agency shall provide to a consumer in
writing not later than 5 business days after the date of the
reinsertion -

(I)
a statement that the disputed information
has been reinserted;

(II)
the business name and address of any
furnisher of information contacted and the
telephone number of such furnisher, if
reasonably available, or of any furnisher of
information that contacted the consumer

reporting agency, in connection with the reinsertion of such information; and

(III)
a notice that the consumer has the right to add a statement to the consumer's file disputing the accuracy or completeness of the disputed information.

(C) Procedures to prevent reappearance

A consumer reporting agency shall maintain reasonable

procedures designed to prevent the reappearance in a

consumer's file, and in consumer reports on the consumer, of

information that is deleted pursuant to this paragraph (other

than information that is reinserted in accordance with

subparagraph (B)(i)).

(6) Notice of results of reinvestigation
(A) In general

A consumer reporting agency shall provide written notice to

a consumer of the results of a reinvestigation under this

subsection not later than 5 business days after the

completion of the reinvestigation, by mail or, if authorized by

the consumer for that purpose, by other means available to

the agency.

(B) Contents

As part of, or in addition to, the notice under subparagraph

(A), a consumer reporting agency shall provide to a

consumer in writing before the expiration of the 5-day period

referred to in subparagraph (A) -

> (i)
> a statement that the reinvestigation is
> completed;

> (ii)
> a consumer report that is based upon the consumer's file as
> that file is revised as a result of the reinvestigation;

> (iii)
> a notice that, if requested by the consumer, a description of
> the procedure used to determine the accuracy and
> completeness of the information shall be provided to the
> consumer by the agency, including the business name and
> address of any furnisher of information contacted in
> connection with such information and the telephone number
> of such furnisher, if reasonably available;

> (iv)
> a notice that the consumer has the right to add a statement
> to the consumer's file disputing the accuracy or
> completeness of the information; and

> (v)
> a notice that the consumer has the right to request under
> subsection (d) of this section that the consumer reporting
> agency furnish notifications under that subsection.

(7) Description of reinvestigation procedure

A consumer reporting agency shall provide to a consumer a

description referred to in paragraph (6)(B)(iii) by not later than 15 days after receiving a request from the consumer for

that description.

(8) Expedited dispute resolution

If a dispute regarding an item of information in a consumer's

file at a consumer reporting agency is resolved in accordance

with paragraph (5)(A) by the deletion of the disputed

information by not later than 3 business days after the date

on which the agency receives notice of the dispute from the

consumer in accordance with paragraph (1)(A), then the

agency shall not be required to comply with paragraphs (2),

(6), and (7) with respect to that dispute if the agency -

(A)

provides prompt notice of the deletion to the consumer by
telephone;

(B)

includes in that notice, or in a written notice that
accompanies a confirmation and consumer report provided in
accordance with subparagraph (C), a statement of the
consumer's right to request under subsection (d) of this
section that the agency furnish notifications under that
subsection; and

(C)

provides written confirmation of the deletion and a copy of a

consumer report on the consumer that is based on the

consumer's file after the deletion, not later than 5 business

days after making the deletion.

(b) Statement of dispute

If the reinvestigation does not resolve the dispute, the consumer may file a brief statement setting forth the nature of the dispute. The consumer reporting agency may limit such statements to not more than one hundred words if it provides the consumer with assistance in writing a clear summary of the dispute.

(c) Notification of consumer dispute in subsequent consumer reports

Whenever a statement of a dispute is filed, unless there is reasonable grounds to believe that it is frivolous or irrelevant, the consumer reporting agency shall, in any subsequent consumer report containing the information in question, clearly note that it is disputed by the consumer and provide either the consumer's statement or a clear and accurate codification or summary thereof.

(d) Notification of deletion of disputed information

Following any deletion of information which is found to be inaccurate or whose accuracy can no longer be verified or any notation as to disputed information, the consumer reporting agency shall, at the request of the consumer, furnish notification that the item has been deleted or the statement, codification or summary pursuant to subsection (b) or (c) of this section to any person specifically designated by the consumer who has within two years prior thereto received a consumer report for employment purposes, or within six months prior thereto received a consumer report for any other purpose, which contained the deleted or disputed information

GLOSSARY

GLOSSARY

GLOSSARY

Credit Agency
The Credit Agency is a free credit reference point designed to aid businesses and consumers in making informed decisions across every area of the Credit Management function from debt collection to credit reporting and credit control to invoice finance

Credit Bureau
A credit rating agency, credit reporting agency (CRA), or credit bureau (U.S.), or credit reference agency (UK) is a company that assigns credit ratings for corporations and individuals. A credit rating measures credit worthiness, the ability to pay back a loan, and affects .

Credit File
See credit record

Credit Record
Credit history or credit report is, in many countries, a record of an individual's or company's past borrowing and repaying, including information about late payments and bankruptcy. The term "credit reputation" can either be used synonymous to *credit history* or to *credit score*

Creditor
A creditor is a party (e.g. person, organization, company, or government) that claims that a second party owes the first party some properties or services. The first party, in general, has provided some property or service to the second party under the assumption (usually enforced

Bankruptcy
A Bankruptcy is a legally declared inability or impairment of ability of an individual or organization to pay their creditors. A declared state of bankruptcy can be requested by creditors in an effort to recoup a portion of what they are owed; however, in the overwhelming majority

Discharged bankruptcy is when you complete all payments, and you are in the clear

Dismissed bankruptcy is when you did not complete the terms of the bankruptcy, and the judge dismissed it.

FACT ACT
Under the Fair and Accurate Credit Transactions Act of 2003 (FACT Act or FACTA), (Public Law 108-159) which was passed by Congress on December 4, of 2003 as an amendment to the Fair Credit Reporting Act, consumers can request and obtain a free credit report once every twelve

FICO
FICO is a mathematical model created by the Experian credit bureau as a tool for lenders to use in evaluating the risk associated with lending you money. Fair Isaac Corporation, or its credit score known as *FICO score* • Flight Information and Control of Operations

Financial Institution
In Financial economics, a financial institution acts as an agent that provides financial services for its clients. Financial institutions generally fall under financial regulation from a government authority. Common types of financial institutions include banks, building societies Example bank or credit union

FCRA

The FCRA stands for the Fair Credit Reporting Act. The FCRA is Federal guidelines for people who grant credit and conduct background investigations for employment purposes.

FTC

The Federal Trade Commission (or FTC) is an independent agency of the United States government, established in 1914 by the Federal Trade Commission Act. Its principal mission is the promotion of consumer protection and the elimination and prevention of anticompetitive business

Secured Credit Card

A secured credit card is a type of credit card secured by a deposit account owned by the cardholder. Typically, the cardholder must deposit between 100% and 200% of the total amount of credit desired

REFERENCES

http://www.consumerinfo.com/n/expsam.htm
http://www.myfico.org
http://www.ftc.gov
http://www.experian.com
http://www.equifax.com
http://www.transunion.com

The last few pages of this booklet contain some of the rules governing the credit bureaus. For more information on FTC rules and regulations go to www.ftc.gov